MONSTER MATH

Frank Schaffer
An imprint of Carson-Dellosa Publishing LLC
Greensboro, North Carolina

MW00896062

Frank Schaffer Publications®
An imprint of Carson-Dellosa Publishing LLC
P.O. Box 35665
Greensboro, NC 27425 USA

© 2010 Carson-Dellosa Publishing LLC. The purchase of this material entitles the buyer to reproduce worksheets and activities for classroom use only—not for commercial resale. Reproduction of these materials for an entire school or district is prohibited. No part of this book may be reproduced (except as noted above), stored in a retrieval system, or transmitted in any form or by any means (mechanically, electronically, recording, etc.) without the prior written consent of Carson-Dellosa Publishing LLC. Frank Schaffer is an imprint of Carson-Dellosa Publishing LLC.

Printed in the USA • All rights reserved.   ISBN 0-7682-4021-2

1 2 3 4 5 6 7 8 9 10 GLO 15 14 13 12 11 10

TABLE OF CONTENTS

Dear Educator,

Congratulations on purchasing the best in educational materials from Frank Schaffer Publications. *Monster Math* is a fun way for young learners to practice and enhance math skills.

The *Monster Math* activities are divided into six skill sets: Numbers & Operations; Geometry; Measurement; Data Analysis & Probability; Algebra; and Problem Solving. These skill sets are correlated to NCTM (National Council of Teachers of Mathematics) standards. There is an assessment at the end of each section entitled Monster Math Drill. These pages will enable young learners to check their progress within each skill set. There is also an answer key at the end of the book.

Our goal in *Monster Math* is to make learning mathematics and problem solving skills fun. We hope young learners will enjoy the activities while gaining knowledge.

Sincerely,
Frank Schaffer Publications

Name: _____

Directions: Count the monsters. Write the number on the line.

_____

1.

_____

2.

_____

3.

_____

4.

_____

5.

_____

Do More: Practice counting out loud. Count objects at home or in your classroom.

Monster Math Grade 1

MONSTER MATCHING

Name: _____

Directions: Draw a line to connect each set of dots with the number and matching number word. The first one has been done for you.

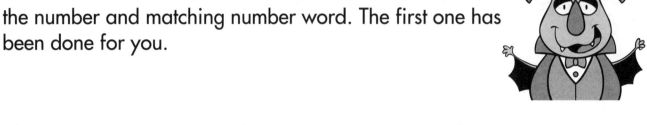

10   nine

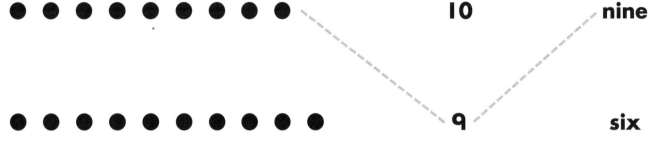

9   six

3   five

7   three

5   seven

6   ten

Do More: Make flash cards using the vocabulary cards in the back of the book. Use the number cards to practice matching number words.

Name: _____

There is more than one way to show a number.
A number can be a **numeral,** a **word,** or a **picture**.

12	twelve	▭▭▭ ▢ ▢
numeral	**word**	**picture**

Directions: Show each number 3 different ways.

1. numeral 6

word _____

picture ▢ ▢ ▢ ▢ ▢ ▢

2. numeral _____

word twelve

picture ▭▭▭▭▭▭▭▭▭ ▢ ▢

3. numeral 13

word _____

picture

4. numeral _____

word eleven

picture

The hungry mouth always opens to more!
Use > for **greater than** and < for **less than**.

🍪 🍪 2 < 4 🍪 🍪 🍪 🍪

Two is **less than** four.

🍪 🍪 🍪 🍪 4 > 2 🍪 🍪

Four is **greater than** two.

Directions: Greater than or less than? Put the right sign in each row.

1. 🍎 🍎 🍎 🍎 🍎 🍎 🍎   7 ☐ 4   🍎 🍎 🍎 🍎

2. 🍌 🍌 🍌 🍌 🍌   5 ☐ 12

3. 🥕🥕🥕🥕🥕🥕🥕🥕🥕🥕🥕🥕🥕🥕🥕🥕   16 ☐ 3

4.    12 ☐ 20

Do More: Say each equation out loud. Use complete sentences.
Example: Seven apples is greater than four apples.

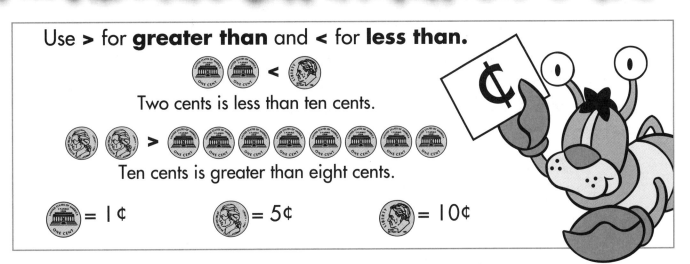

Use **>** for **greater than** and **<** for **less than**.

Two cents is less than ten cents.

Ten cents is greater than eight cents.

= 1 ¢   = 5¢   = 10¢

Directions: Write how many cents. Which side has more money? Fill in a greater than (**>**) or less than (**<**) sign.

1. [ ]

2. [ ]

3.   [ ]

4.   [ ]

Do More: Use pennies, nickels, and dimes to make a new equation. Have a friend tell which sign should be used—greater than or less than.

Monster Math Grade 1

EVEN AND ODD NUMBERS

Name: _____

Directions: Which are the **even** numbers? Start at number 2. Use a red crayon to circle every other number. Which are the **odd** numbers? Start at number 1. Use a blue crayon to put an **X** over every other number. To prove your work, be sure the red circles and the blue **X**s are lined up in columns.

1	2	3	4	5	6	7	8	9	10
11	12	13	14	15	16	17	18	19	20
21	22	23	24	25	26	27	28	29	30
31	32	33	34	35	36	37	38	39	40
41	42	43	44	45	46	47	48	49	50
51	52	53	54	55	56	57	58	59	60
61	62	63	64	65	66	67	68	69	70
71	72	73	74	75	76	77	78	79	80
81	82	83	84	85	86	87	88	89	90
91	92	93	94	95	96	97	98	99	100

Do More: Use the chart to count the numbers from 1 to 100 out loud.

COUNTING BY TWOS

Name: _____

Directions: Another way of counting by even numbers is counting by twos. Fill in the missing numbers.

1 _____ 3 _____ 5 _____ 7 _____ 9 _____

11 _____ 13 _____ 15 _____ 17 _____ 19 _____

21 _____ 23 _____ 25 _____ 27 _____ 29 _____

31 _____ 33 _____ 35 _____ 37 _____ 39 _____

41 _____ 43 _____ 45 _____ 47 _____ 49 _____

Do More: Count out loud by twos from 2 to 100 (even numbers). Then, count out loud by twos from 1 to 99 (odd numbers).

Monster Math Grade 1

Directions: In each group, write the missing number on the line.

_____

- - - - - - - - - - -

1. 6 _____ 8

_____

- - - - - - - - - - -

2. 62 _____ 64

_____

- - - - - - - - - - -

3. 20 _____ 22

6. 85 _____ 87

_____

- - - - - - - - - - -

4. 94 _____ 96

7. 32 _____ 34

_____

- - - - - - - - - - -

5. 9 _____ 11

8. 91 _____ 93

Do More: Find a friend. Name an even number. Your friend tells the next even number that follows. Then, have your friend name an odd number. You tell the next odd number that follows.

COUTING BY FIVES

Directions: Circle every number that ends with a 5 or a 0. Watch the pattern that develops. The first row has been done for you.

1	2	3	4	(5)	6	7	8	9	(10)
11	12	13	14	15	16	17	18	19	20
21	22	23	24	25	26	27	28	29	30
31	32	33	34	35	36	37	38	39	40
41	42	43	44	45	46	47	48	49	50
51	52	53	54	55	56	57	58	59	60
61	62	63	64	65	66	67	68	69	70
71	72	73	74	75	76	77	78	79	80
81	82	83	84	85	86	87	88	89	90
91	92	93	94	95	96	97	98	99	100

Do More: Use this page to help you count out loud from 5 to 100.

Name: _____

Directions: In each row, color the first monster purple and the last monster orange.

Directions: Number the monsters in line. Match each monster to the word that tells where it is in line.

third

first

second

fourth

Do More: How else could you describe the fourth monster in line on this page? How about the third monster in line?

Monster Math Grade 1

ONE HALF

Name: _____

Directions: Color one half ($\frac{1}{2}$) of each shape.

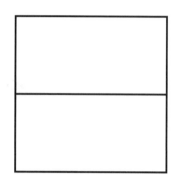  

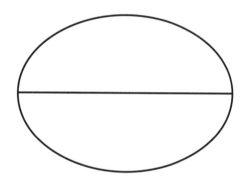 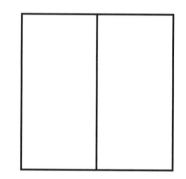

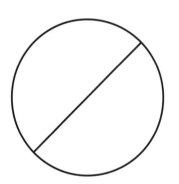 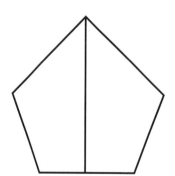 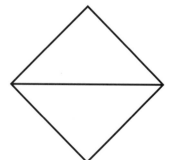

Do More: Cut circles, squares, triangles, and rectangles from colored paper. Fold them in half. What shape is half of a square? Is there more than one way to cut a square in half? Can you cut a square in half so that you end up with 2 triangles?

Name: _____

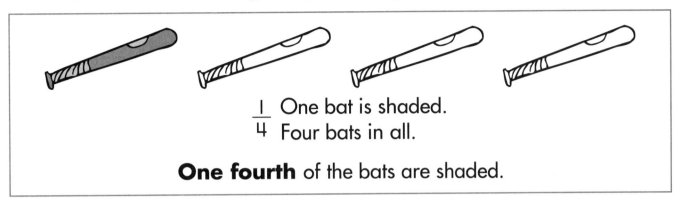

$\frac{1}{4}$ One bat is shaded.
Four bats in all.

One fourth of the bats are shaded.

Directions: Color **one fourth** ($\frac{1}{4}$) of the balls in each group.

1.

2.

3.

4.

Monster Math Grade 1

Name: _____

 One book is colored.
Three books in all.

One third of the books are colored.

Directions: Does the picture show **one third** ($\frac{1}{3}$)? Circle yes or no.

Check your work. Pictures that show $\frac{1}{3}$ will have 1 part colored, 3 parts in all.

I.   **yes**   **no**

2.   **yes**   **no**

3.   **yes**   **no**

4.    **yes**   **no**

Do More: Count out 6 objects. Divide them in half. How many in each pile? Put them back in one pile again. Now divide the 6 objects into 3 equal groups. Which is more—one third or one half?

Monster Math Grade 1

Name: _____

Directions: Count the dots on each monster. Solve each problem.

_____

----

1. $6 + 1 = 7$

_____

----

2. $4 + 4 =$ _____

_____

----

3. $2 + 6 =$ _____

_____

----

4. $5 + 4 =$ _____

_____

----

5. $3 + 6 =$ _____

6. $5 + 2 =$ _____

Monster Math Grade 1

PROVING THE FACTS-ADDITION Name: _____

Directions: Look at the equations. Circle the right number of dots to prove the equations are equal. The first one has been done for you.

1. 5 + 6 = _____ ⬤ ⬤ ⬤ ⬤ ⬤ ⬤ ⬤ ⬤ ⬤ ⬤ ⬤

6 + 5 = _____ ⬤ ⬤ ⬤ ⬤ ⬤ ⬤ ⬤ ⬤ ⬤ ⬤ ⬤

2. 4 + 8 = _____ ⬤ ⬤ ⬤ ⬤ ⬤ ⬤ ⬤ ⬤ ⬤ ⬤ ⬤ ⬤

8 + 4 = _____ ⬤ ⬤ ⬤ ⬤ ⬤ ⬤ ⬤ ⬤ ⬤ ⬤ ⬤ ⬤

3. 3 + 11 = _____ ⬤ ⬤ ⬤ ⬤ ⬤ ⬤ ⬤ ⬤ ⬤ ⬤ ⬤ ⬤ ⬤ ⬤

11 + 3 = _____ ⬤ ⬤ ⬤ ⬤ ⬤ ⬤ ⬤ ⬤ ⬤ ⬤ ⬤ ⬤ ⬤ ⬤

4. 6 + 7 = _____ ⬤ ⬤ ⬤ ⬤ ⬤ ⬤ ⬤ ⬤ ⬤ ⬤ ⬤ ⬤ ⬤

7 + 6 = _____ ⬤ ⬤ ⬤ ⬤ ⬤ ⬤ ⬤ ⬤ ⬤ ⬤ ⬤ ⬤ ⬤

Name: _____

Directions: Solve each problem by crossing out the number taken away. The first one has been done for you.

1. 5 – 2 = 3

2. 4 – 1 = _____

3. 6 – 3 = _____

4. 8 – 4 = _____

5. 7 – 5 = _____

6. 9 – 3 = _____

Monster Math Grade 1

Name: _____

Directions: Find the difference. Cross out the bubbles being taken away. Then, count the bubbles that are left to prove your answer.

1. 10 – 5 = _____

2. 7 – 6 = _____

4. 5 – 1 = _____

3. 9 – 6 = _____

5. 6 – 4 = _____

Do More: Draw a picture with some bubbles crossed out. Then, write the number problem for the picture.

Name: _____

Directions: Answer the questions to review the skills you have learned.

1. Circle the even numbers.

2   5   8   11   18   20

2. Circle the odd numbers.

2   6   9   11   15   21

_____   _____

3. Counting by 2s,   ---------------   **4.** Counting by 5s,   ---------------
what number comes   what number comes
after 16?   _____   after 60?   _____

5. Write the number for each of these words.

_____   _____

----------------------------   ----------------------------

one _____   eleven _____

_____   _____

----------------   ----------------

6. Write the number   **7.** Write the number
that comes after 8.   _____   that comes before 48. _____

8. Use a picture and word to show the number two more ways.

14 _____

Monster Math Grade 1

9. Use the sign **>**, **<**, or **=** to complete the number sentences.

5 ☐ 8   11 ☐ 9   15 ☐ 15

10. Color the part of the shape that matches each fraction.

$\frac{1}{3}$  $\frac{1}{2}$  $\frac{1}{4}$ ☐

11. Write the number that will continue the pattern.

_____

- - - - - - - - - - - - - - -

2   4   6   8   10   12   14   _____

12. Circle the first monster. Cross out the last monster. Draw a box around the second monster. Draw a triangle around the third monster.

13. Find the sum.

_____

- - - - - - - - - - -

3 + 1 = _____

14. Find the difference.

_____

- - - - - - - - - - -

5 − 3 = _____

This is a **square**.

It has 4 sides.

All the sides are the same length.

Directions: Look at all the shapes. Color the squares red.

This is a **triangle**.

It has 3 sides.

Directions: Look at all the shapes. Color the triangles blue.

Name: _____

This is a **rectangle**.

It has 4 sides.

Directions: Look at all the shapes. Color the rectangles green.

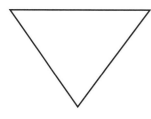
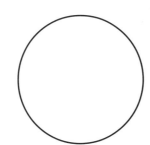

Monster Math Grade 1

Name: _____

This is a **circle**.

It is round.

It has no sides.

Directions: Look at all the shapes. Color the circles orange.

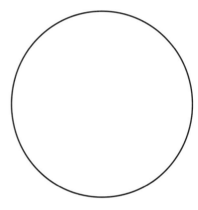

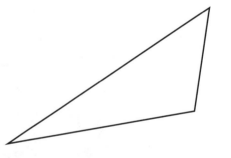

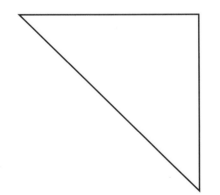

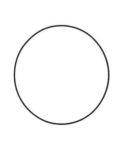

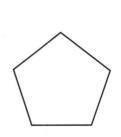

Drawing Lines

A **line** goes on in both directions without ending.

Arrows are on both ends to show that the line goes on.

Directions: Trace the dashed line segments to draw each line. Trace the arrows on both ends.

1.

2.

3.

4.

Name: _____

Directions: Draw a line to match each shape to its name.

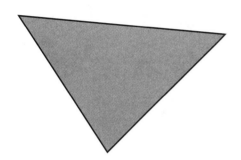

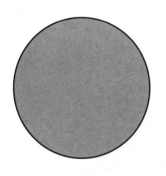

circle

triangle

square

rectangle

SIDING WITH A SHAPE

Name: _____

Directions: Answer each question.

1. How many sides does a square have?

_____

2. How many sides does a triangle have?

_____

3. How many sides does a rectangle have?

_____

4. How many sides does a circle have?

_____

5. Are all rectangles the same size?

_____

6. If one side of a square is 5 inches, what is the length of the other 3 sides?

_____

Monster Math Grade 1

Name: _____

A **solid figure** is a 3-dimensional shape.

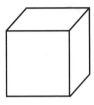
cube

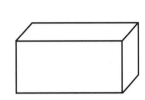
rectangular prism

cone

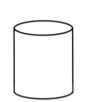
cylinder

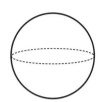
sphere

Directions: Write the name under each figure.

1.
_____

- - - - - - - - - - - - - - - -

2.
_____

- - - - - - - - - - - - - - - -

3.
_____

- - - - - - - - - - - - - - - -

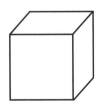
4.
_____

- - - - - - - - - - - - - - - -

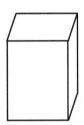
5.
_____

- - - - - - - - - - - - - - - -

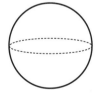
6.
_____

- - - - - - - - - - - - - - - -

X Marks the Figure

Name: _____

Directions: Put an **X** on each of the solid figures.

Monster Math Grade 1

Directions: Read the map of Monster Town. Circle the correct answer for each question.

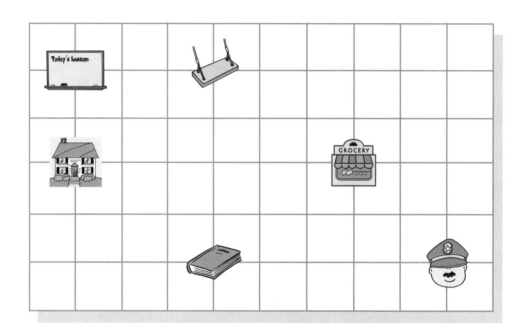

1. is _____ of [Today's Lesson]   **right**   **left**

2. [GROCERY] is _____ of [house]   **right**   **left**

3. [book] is _____ of [police officer]   **right**   **left**

4. [Today's Lesson] is _____ of [swing]   **right**   **left**

Name: _____

Directions: Monsters love fruit. Fill in each blank with the word **right** or **left**.

apple

banana

grapes

lemon

peach

_____

1. The apple is _____ of the lemon.

_____

2. The grapes are _____ of the banana.

_____

3. The peach is _____ of the lemon.

_____

4. The banana is _____ of the apple.

35

Name: _____

Directions: Use the list of numbers to answer each question.

1	15	29	43	57
50	39	26	13	0
4	16	28	40	52

8

34

1. What number is above 26?

_____

_____

2. What number is above 13?

_____

_____

3. What number is below 50?

_____

_____

4. What number is below 0?

_____

_____

5. Name a number above 16.

_____

_____

6. Name a number below 43.

_____

_____

Name: _____

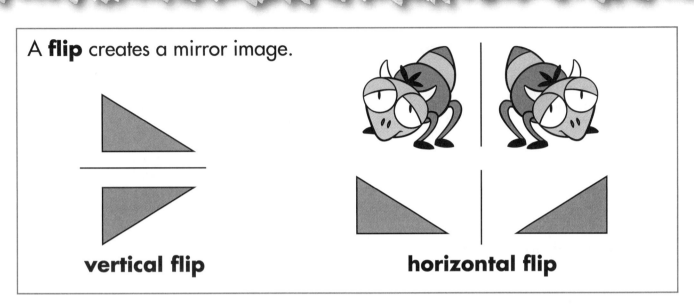

A **flip** creates a mirror image.

vertical flip

horizontal flip

Directions: Decide if a horizontal flip, a vertical flip, or no flip is shown. Circle the correct answer.

1.

horizontal flip   vertical flip   no flip

2.

horizontal flip   vertical flip   no flip

3.

horizontal flip   vertical flip   no flip

4.

horizontal flip   vertical flip   no flip

A **slide** creates the same image in a different place.

Directions: Draw a slide of each in the directions given.

1. slide right and down

2. slide up and left

3. slide left

4. slide right and down

Do More: Which object looks the same after a flip as it does after the slide?

Name: _____

A **turn** rotates an image.

clockwise

counterclockwise

Directions: Decide if each turn is clockwise or counterclockwise. Circle the correct answer.

1. **B ꓭ**   **clockwise**   **counterclockwise**

2. **Y ⅄**   **clockwise**   **counterclockwise**

3. **J ⌐**   **clockwise**   **counterclockwise**

4. **E ⱻ**   **clockwise**   **counterclockwise**

5. **G ⅁**   **clockwise**   **counterclockwise**

Monster Math Grade 1

MOVING LETTERS

Name: _____

Directions: Flip, slide, and turn each letter given. Then, complete the chart below by drawing how each letter looks.

	Flip it. (horizontal)	Slide it.	Turn it. (clockwise)
T			
M			
P			
K			

Do More: Choose one of the letters above. Show its vertical flip and its counterclockwise turn.

Name: _____

Directions: Circle the solid figure that each object models.

1.

2.

3.

Do More: Sketch a picture of an object that models a cone.

Monster Math Grade 1

NAME SOLID FIGURES

Directions: Write the name of each solid figure.
Choose from the names listed below.

cone   cube   cylinder

rectangular prism   sphere

1.

_____

- - - - - - - - - - - - - - - -

_____

2.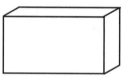

_____

- - - - - - - - - - - - - - - -

_____

3.

_____

- - - - - - - - - - - - - - - -

_____

4.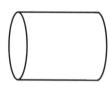

_____

- - - - - - - - - - - - - - - -

_____

5.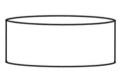

_____

- - - - - - - - - - - - - - - -

_____

6.

_____

- - - - - - - - - - - - - - - -

_____

Name: _____

Directions: Answer the questions to review the skills you have learned.

1. Draw a line.

2. Circle the name of this shape.

circle
square
triangle

3. Is this a 2-dimensional figure or a 3-dimensional figure? Circle the correct answer.

2-dimensional figure
3-dimensional figure

4. Circle the object that is to the right of the .

Monster Math Grade 1

5. Draw a circle under this rectangle.

6. When the 2 shapes below are put together, which shape is formed? Circle the correct answer.

7. Which transformation is shown? Circle the correct answer.

slide

flip

turn

8. What shape is the mirror in this picture?

_____

- -

_____

Name: _____

Directions: Write **L** by the longer object. Write **S** by the shorter object.

1.

2.

3.

4.

Play a game with a friend. Each person finds an object. Show your objects to each other. One of you will say, "Mine is longer." The other one will say, "Mine is shorter." Play again several times.

Do More: When is the word **taller** better than the word **longer**?

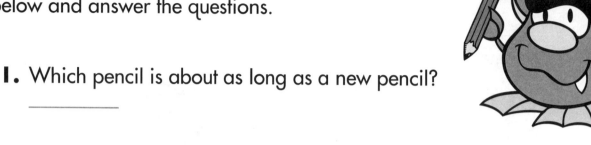

Directions: Look at Merry Monster's pencil collection below and answer the questions.

1. Which pencil is about as long as a new pencil?

_____

- - - - - - - - - - - -

_____

2. Put Merry's pencils in order from shortest to longest.

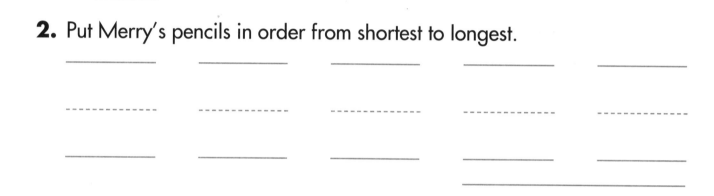

3. Which pencils are shorter than a new pencil? _____

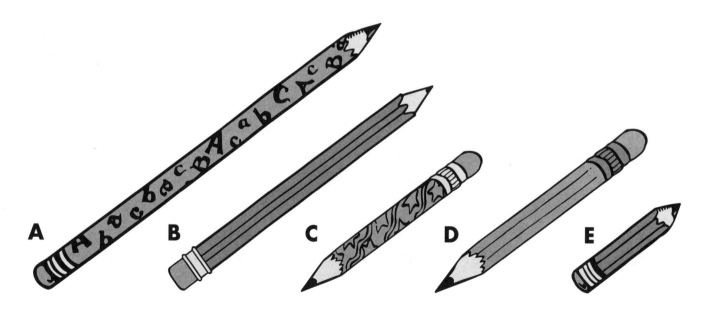

A   B   C   D   E

How Much Does It Hold?

Name: _____

Directions: Write **M** by the one that holds **more**.
Write **L** by the one that holds **less**.

1. _ _ _ _ _ _ _ _ _ _ _ _    _ _ _ _ _ _ _ _ _ _ _ _

2. _ _ _ _ _ _ _ _ _ _ _ _    _ _ _ _ _ _ _ _ _ _ _ _

3. _ _ _ _ _ _ _ _ _ _ _ _   _ _ _ _ _ _ _ _ _ _ _ _

4.  _ _ _ _ _ _ _ _ _ _ _ _   _ _ _ _ _ _ _ _ _ _ _ _

5. Find four containers. Put them in order from **holds the least** to **holds the most**.

Do More: How can you prove which container holds more or less?

Monster Math Grade 1

WHAT IS MASS?

Name: _____

Directions: Hold something different in each hand. Which object seems to pull on your hand more? This is the heavier object. It has more mass than the other one. Circle the one in each pair that has more mass.

1.

2.

3.

4.

5. A balance scale shows which one is heavier. Draw two things on the scale. Which side should the heavier one go on?

Name: _____

Directions: Answer the questions.

1. Look at the three objects below. Which do you think is heaviest? Which is lightest? Which is in the middle? Number them 1–3 to show lightest to heaviest.

_____   _____   _____

- - - - - - - - -   - - - - - - - - -   - - - - - - - - -

_____   _____   _____

2. Choose three items. Guess what order they go in.
Guess:

lightest   **heaviest**

Prove it. Weigh the objects.
Actual:

lightest   **heaviest**

Monster Math Grade 1

COUNTING UNITS

Name: _____

Directions: Answer the questions.

1. Tell about the size of this pencil.

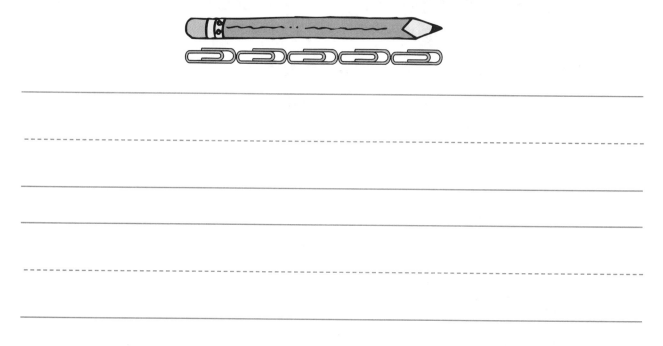

_____

- -

_____

_____

- -

_____

2. Do these marbles help you tell about the size of this pencil? Why?

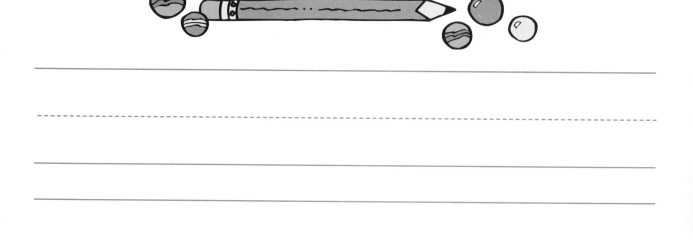

_____

- -

_____

_____

- -

_____

Name: _____

Directions: Answer the questions.

1. Tell about the size of the scissors.

_____

- -

_____

_____

- -

_____

2. Do these stamps help tell about the size of this crayon? Explain.

_____

- -

_____

_____

- -

_____

WHAT IS AREA?

Name: _____

Directions: This monster is making a paper quilt. He will cover his paper with rows of squares. He needs to know how many squares he wants. Can you help him figure it out?

Look at the paper. Look at the size of the square.

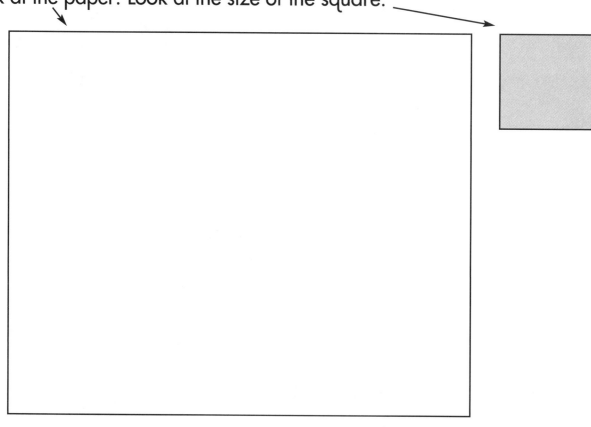

1. How many squares cover the paper? _____

2. The area of the paper is _____ squares.

Do More: Make a quilt with colored paper. Cut out colored squares and glue them in a pattern.

COUNTING MINUTES

Directions: Look at the clock. There are 60 marks around the edge. There are 60 minutes in an hour. The long hand on a clock points to these marks. When it points straight up, it is at 0 (or o'clock). Count around each clock to the minute hand. Write the number of minutes on the line.

Example:    0 minutes

1.

_____
- - - - - - - - - - -
_____ minutes

2.

_____
- - - - - - - - - - -
_____ minutes

3.

_____
- - - - - - - - - - -
_____ minutes

4.

_____
- - - - - - - - - - -
_____ minutes

Monster Math Grade 1

Name: _____

Directions: How long is each thing?

1.

_____

- - - - - - - - - - - - -

_____ paper clips

2.

_____

- - - - - - - - - - - -

_____ paper clips

3.

_____

- - - - - - - - - - - -

_____ paper clips

4.

_____

- - - - - - - - - - - -

_____ paper clips

Do More: Make your own measuring tool. You need a strip of cardboard and about 10 paper clips. Tape the paper clips along the edge of the cardboard. Make sure the ends touch. Measure four things from your desk. Line up the item with the end of one paper clip.

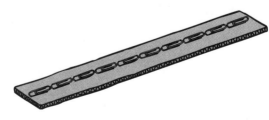

Name: _____

Directions: Answer the questions.

1. How big is this shape? Count how many squares it covers.

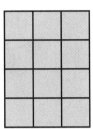 

_____

- - - - - - - - - - - - - - -

_____ squares

2. I cut the shape. It changes. Is it still the same size? Count how many squares it covers now.

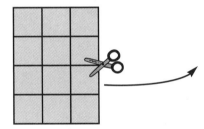 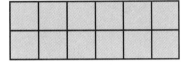

_____

- - - - - - - - - - - - - - -

_____ squares

3. I cut the shape. It changes. Is it still the same size? Count how many squares it covers now.

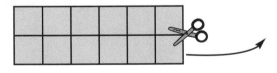 

_____

- - - - - - - - - - - - - - -

_____ squares

Do More: Tell why the different rectangles cover the same space. Will this be true with other shapes?

Directions: Which tool can you use to measure? Circle the best choice.

1. How much does this jar hold?

2. How tall is this monster?

3. How much water?

4. How heavy is this bag of candy?

5. How short is this book?

Name: _____

Directions: Look at this jar of paint. The numbers tell you how much paint there is.

1. Dan needs 5 cups of paint to cover the wall he is

_____

----

painting. Is this enough paint? _____

2. Brad needs 3 cups of paint. This is . . .
   a. too little paint.
   b. too much paint.
   c. just the right amount.

Directions: Look at this jar of rice. The numbers tell you how much there is.

_____

----

3. Fen needs 3 cups of rice. Is there enough? _____

_____

----

4. Tia needs 5 cups of rice. Is this too little rice? _____
Why is it hard to tell?

Monster Math Grade 1

Name: _____

Directions: Fill in the missing numbers on the rulers.
How long is each object?

_____

- - - - - - - - - - - - - -

1. The pen is _____ inches long.

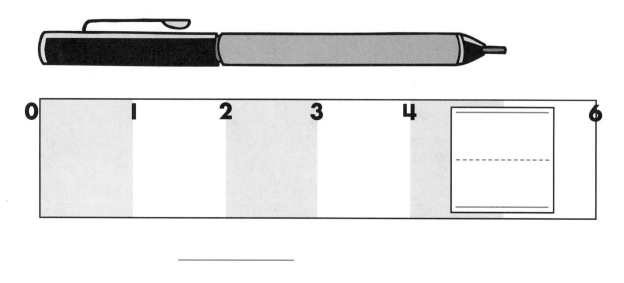

| 0 | I | 2 | 3 | 4 | | 6 |

_____

- - - - - - - - - - - - - -

2. The shovel is _____ inches long.

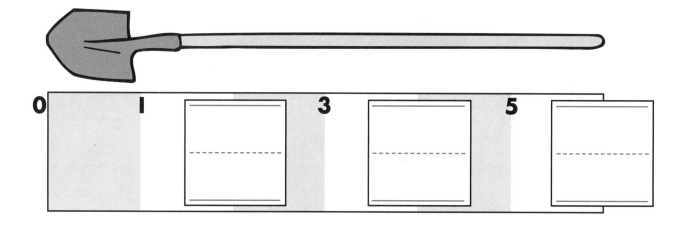

| 0 | I | | 3 | | 5 | |

FINDING CENTIMETERS

Name: _____

Directions: Use your centimeter ruler to measure many things. How high can you go? Write what you find in the chart.

Object	Measurement (cm)
button	1 cm
stamp	2 cm
	3 cm
	4 cm
	5 cm
	6 cm
	7 cm
	8 cm
	9 cm
	10 cm
	11 cm
	12 cm

Do More: Can you find something that is about 50 cm? Guess and check.

Directions: Measure the plant to the closest measurement. Use inches and centimeters.

Stem A

_____   _____

- - - - - - - - - - - -   - - - - - - - - - - - -

Inches _____   Centimeters _____

Leaf A

_____   _____

- - - - - - - - - - - -   - - - - - - - - - - - -

Inches _____   Centimeters _____

Stem B

_____

- - - - - - - - - - - -

Inches _____

_____

- - - - - - - - - - - -

Centimeters _____

Leaf B

_____

- - - - - - - - - - - -

Inches _____

_____

- - - - - - - - - - - -

Centimeters _____

Leaf B

Leaf A

Stem B

Stem A

Name: _____

Directions: Look at a calendar for this month.

1. What month is it right now?

_____

- -

_____

_____

- -

2. How many Mondays are in this month? _____

_____

- -

3. How many Saturdays are in this month? _____

_____

- -

4. What is the number of the first Wednesday this month? _____

_____

- -

5. What is the number of the third Thursday this month? _____

Monster Math Grade 1

Name: _____

Directions: Answer the questions to review the skills you have learned.

1. Circle the pencil that is longer.

2. Circle the foot that is shorter.

3. Circle the monster that is fatter.

4. Circle the glass that holds more water.

5. Circle the marble that is lighter.

6. About what time is it?  **3:50**   **7:30**   **9:00**

Name: _____

7. Look at the scale. How many blocks

_____

- - - - - - - - - - - - - -

equal the mass of the monster? _____

8. 

    scale   **ruler**   **cup**   **clock**

Which is the best tool for measuring . . .

_____

- -

a. how long it takes to get to school? _____

_____

- -

b. the weight of a shoe? _____

63

Odd Shape Out

Name: _____

Directions: Put an **X** on the shape that does not belong.

1.

2.

3.

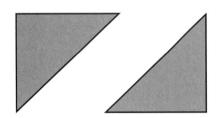 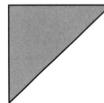 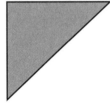 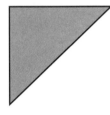

4.

  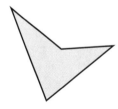 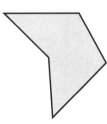 

Do More: Choose one group of shapes. Tell why the shape does not belong.

Name: _____

Directions: Circle the monster that does not go in each group.

Name: _____

Directions: Help Lizzy Monster sort the word. Write 2 words from the list that match each.

house   cake   room   work

truck   walk   book   show

1. has an o

_____

_____

_____

2. is a 5 letter word

_____

_____

_____

3. ends with an e

_____

_____

_____

4. has a k

_____

_____

_____

Name: _____

A **set** is a group of information. A set can be numbers, names, or things. There are 5 squares in this set. ☐☐☐☐☐

Directions: Tell how many are in each set.

1. 2, 3, 4, 5

_____

- - - - - - - - - - - - - - - - - -

_____

2. Bob, Ann, Jim

_____

- - - - - - - - - - - - - - - - - -

_____

3. 1, 1, 5, 5, 9, 10

_____

- - - - - - - - - - - - - - - - - -

_____

4. apple, orange, peach, peach

_____

- - - - - - - - - - - - - - - - - -

_____

5. pen, pencil, chalk, pen

_____

- - - - - - - - - - - - - - - - - -

_____

6.

_____

- - - - - - - - - - - - - - - - - -

_____

Monster Math Grade 1

Name: _____

A **tally mark** is a way to count.
Tally marks are grouped in sets of 5 to make counting easier.
ⵗⵗ is a group of 5 tally marks.

Directions: Count the tally marks. Write the number for each color.

Favorite Colors		
Color	**Tally**	**Number**
Red	ⵗⵗ ⵗⵗ ‖	
Blue	ⵗⵗ ⵗⵗ ⵗⵗ ∣	
Green	ⵗⵗ ‖‖	
Yellow	ⵗⵗ	
Purple	ⵗⵗ ‖‖	

MONSTER COOKIES

Name: _____

Directions: Monsters love to munch on cookies! Make tally marks for the number on each cookie jar. Color one square for each cookie.

1.

COOKIES 5 _____

2.

COOKIES 3 _____

3.

COOKIES 4 _____

4.

COOKIES 6 _____

Do More: How are the tally marks and the colored squares the same?

Monster Math Grade 1

Is That a Fact?

Name: _____

A **fact** is known to be true.
An example of a fact: The temperature today is 38°F.

An **opinion** tells how a person feels or thinks.
An example of an opinion: Cherry pie tastes good.

Directions: Tell if each is a fact or an opinion. Circle the correct answer.

1. Six children walked to school today.   **fact   opinion**

2. Red is the best color for roses.   **fact   opinion**

3. Bobby is the best on the team.   **fact   opinion**

4. Calli's mother makes the best cookies.   **fact   opinion**

5. Washington D.C. is the nation's capital.   **fact   opinion**

Do More: Write a fact about yourself. Write an opinion about yourself.

Name: _____

Directions: Color each sign that is a fact.

Grapes are fruit.

Ice is frozen.

Babies are cute.

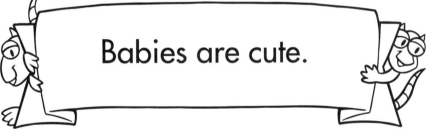

Blue is a color.

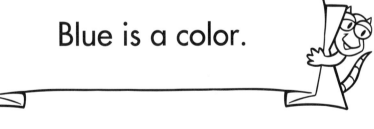

A fly is a bug.

Monster Math Grade 1

Name: _____

A **pictograph** is a way to show data using pictures.

The **key** of the pictograph tells what each picture stands for.

Directions: Use the pictograph to answer the questions on page 73.

Number of Apples Eaten by the Monsters

Scary	🍎 🍎
Scruffy	🍎 🍎 🍎
Fuzzy	🍎
Growly	🍎 🍎 🍎 🍎
Scowly	🍎 🍎

Key: 🍎 = 1 apple

Do More: How many apples did Scary Monster eat if each stands for 2 apples?

Name: _____

Directions: Use the pictograph on page 72 to answer each question.

_____

1. How many apples did Scary Monster eat?

_____

2. Who ate the most apples?

_____

3. Who ate the least apples?

_____

4. How many apples did Scowly Monster eat?

_____

5. Who ate the same number of apples as Scary Monster?

Monster Math Grade 1

MONSTER PICTOGRAPH

Name: _____

Directions: Use the pictograph to answer the questions on page 75.

Books the Monsters Read

Key: = 1 book

Do More: What is the key? What does it mean?

Name: _____

Directions: Use the pictograph on page 74 to answer each question.

1. How many books did  read? _____

2. How many books did read? _____

3. How many books did read? _____

4. How many books did read? _____

5. How many books did read? _____

Do More: What was the least number of books read?

Monster Math Grade 1

Name: _____

Bar graphs show data with horizontal or vertical bars so that readers can more easily compare the data.

Directions: Use the bar graph to answer the questions on page 77.

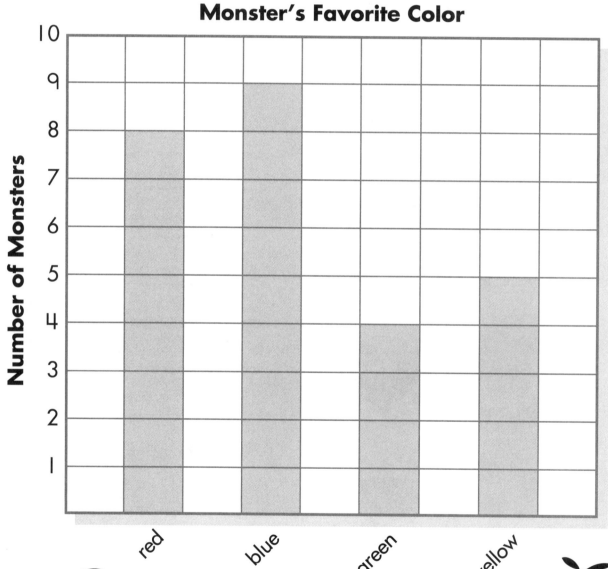

Monster's Favorite Color

Name: _____

Directions: Use the bar graph on page 76 to answer each question.

_____

----

1. How many monsters liked red best?

_____

_____

----

2. How many monsters liked green best?

_____

_____

----

3. How many monsters liked blue best?

_____

_____

----

4. How many monsters liked yellow best?

_____

_____

----

5. Which color was the favorite of most monsters? _____

I like two colors.

Do More: How many monsters were asked in all?

Monster Math Grade 1

THE MODE

Name: _____

Directions: Write the number you see the most in each set.

1. 1, 1, 2, 3, 5, 7, 9

_____

_____

2. 3, 4, 4, 4, 6, 7, 8

_____

_____

3. 1, 1, 4, 7, 7, 7, 10

_____

_____

4. 5, 7, 7, 8, 8, 8, 8, 10

_____

_____

5. 10, 11, 12, 13, 14, 14, 15

_____

Do More: How did you decide for question 4?

Middle Number

When numbers are put in order, the **median** is the number in the middle.

Directions: Write the middle number in the blank.

_____

1. 1, 1, 2, 3, 5

_____

2. 3, 4, 6, 7, 8

_____

3. 10, 12, 14, 17, 19, 21, 30

_____

4. 5, 7, 8, 8, 10

_____

5. 100, 112, 145

Do More: Do all questions 1–5 have an odd number of numbers?

Monster Math Grade 1

Name: _____

An event that can never happen is **impossible**.

An event that might happen is **possible**.

Directions: Tell if each event is impossible or possible. Circle the correct answer.

1. The sun will shine tomorrow.　　　**impossible**　　**possible**

2. The day after Monday is Wednesday.　　**impossible**　　**possible**

3. A cat will square dance.　　　**impossible**　　**possible**

4. You will see a police officer today.　　**impossible**　　**possible**

5. Today will last 36 hours.　　　**impossible**　　**possible**

Do More: Name another event that is impossible.

Name: _____

Directions: Answer the questions to review the skills you have learned. Use the pictograph to answer questions 1–3.

Pet Monsters

Jimmy	🐾 🐾 🐾 🐾
Andrea	🐾 🐾 🐾
Marlo	🐾 🐾
Sahir	🐾 🐾 🐾 🐾

Key: = 1 monster

_____

- - - - - - - - - - - - - - - - - -

1. How many does Jimmy have?_____

- - - - - - - - - - - - - - - - - -

2. Who has the least ?_____

3. Which two children have the same number of 🐾?

_____

- - - - - - - - - - - - - - - - - -

_____

Name: _____

4. Circle the middle number.

2   5   5   7   8

5. Put an **X** on the square that does not belong.

6. Circle the object that is different.

Circle the word that tells about each.

7. You will eat an apple today.

certain   **possible**   **impossible**

8. Thursday will be the day after Wednesday.

certain   **possible**   **impossible**

Directions: Which one is my heart? Listen to the clues.

My heart is not a small heart. Cross out all the small hearts.

My heart is not a striped heart. Cross out all the striped hearts.

My heart is not upside down. Cross out all the upside-down hearts.

Color my heart red.

Do More: Describe how you could sort all the hearts on the page.

Directions: Find the shape pattern in each row. Draw the next shape in each pattern.

1.

2.

3.

4.

Do More: For each pattern, what is the group of shapes that is repeated? Circle one of the groups in each pattern.

Directions: These two patterns are the same. Study the pattern. Then, follow the directions.

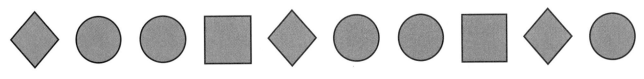

3   4   4   7   3   4   4   7   3   4

1. Use colors to show the same pattern.

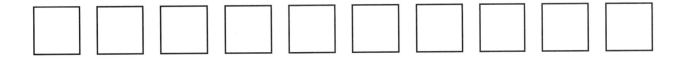

2. Make two new patterns that are the same. Use a number pattern and a color pattern.

_____ _____ _____ _____ _____ _____ _____

- - - - - -   - - - - - -   - - - - - -   - - - - - -   - - - - - -   - - - - - -   - - - - - -

_____ _____ _____ _____ _____ _____ _____

Monster Math Grade 1

Directions: Circle the correct number of monsters to make each statement true.

1.

$9 =$

2.

$7 =$

3.

$10 =$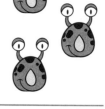

4.

$12 =$

Do More: What does the equal sign tell you about the two things it connects?

Name: _____

Directions: Write a number that makes each sentence true. Then, draw the dots on the monster.

1.

_____

- - - - - - - - - - - -

_____ is less than 7

2.

_____

- - - - - - - - - - - -

_____ is more than 5

3.

_____

- - - - - - - - - - - -

_____ is less than 9

4.

_____

- - - - - - - - - - - -

_____ is more than 8

Monster Math Grade 1

Directions: Help Murray Monster solve the mystery. Read the clues for each problem. Circle all the numbers that solve the mystery.

I. I am > 4. I am < 7. What numbers could I be?

1	2	3	4	5	6	7	8	9	10	11	12	13	14	15

2. I am > 8. I am < 13. What numbers could I be?

1	2	3	4	5	6	7	8	9	10	11	12	13	14	15

3. I am > 1. I am < 6. What numbers could I be?

1	2	3	4	5	6	7	8	9	10	11	12	13	14	15

4. I am > 6. I am < 14. What numbers could I be?

1	2	3	4	5	6	7	8	9	10	11	12	13	14	15

Do More: Make up your own clues about some numbers. Trade clues with a friend and find the mystery numbers.

Directions: Compare the two numbers and color the correct sign.

1.

8  9

4.

4  6

2.

3 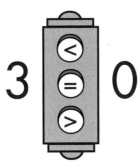 0

5.

5 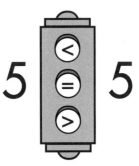 5

3.

6 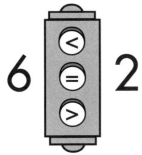 2

6.

4 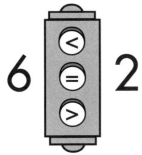 8

Name: _____

Directions: Write **+** to show addition. Write **−** to show subtraction. Write **+** or **−** in the circle to make each number sentence true.

1.

9 ◯ 3 = 12

2.

5 ◯ 4 = 9

3.

11 ◯ 6 = 5

4.

3 ◯ 3 = 0

5.

2 ◯ 6 = 8

Do More: Choose one of the problems. Explain how you decided whether to use the plus sign or the minus sign.

Name: _____

Directions: Answer the questions.

1. Draw blocks to make the scale balance.

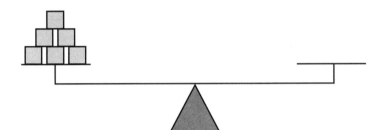

2. Write **+** or **−** to make each number sentence true.

a. 5 ◯ 6 = 11   **c.** 7 ◯ 2 = 5

b. 9 ◯ 2 = 7   **d.** 4 ◯ 6 = 10

3. Write **>** , **<**, or **=**

a. 8 ◯ 5   **c.** 10 ◯ 12

b. 6 ◯ 6   **d.** 7 ◯ 3

4. Circle all the number that could be the mystery number.

a. I am > 8. I am < 13. What numbers could I be?

1	2	3	4	5	6	7	8	9	10	11	12	13	14	15

b. I am > 2. I am < 7. What numbers could I be?

1	2	3	4	5	6	7	8	9	10	11	12	13	14	15

Monster Math Grade 1

Name: _____

Directions: Write the addition sentence shown by the pictures.

1.

_____

- -

_____

2.

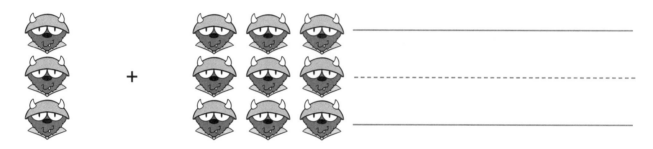

_____

- -

_____

3.

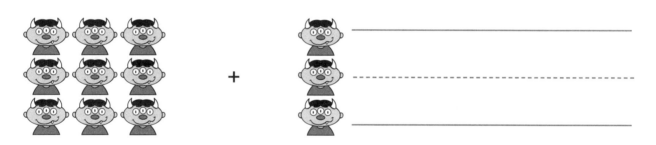

_____

- -

_____

4.

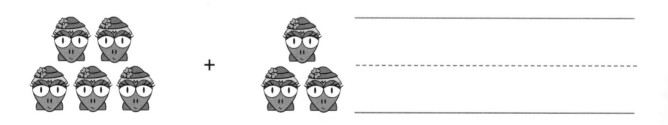

_____

- -

_____

Do More: Read each addition sentence aloud.

SUBTRACTING MONSTERS

Name: _____

Directions: Write the subtraction sentence shown by the pictures.

1.

2.

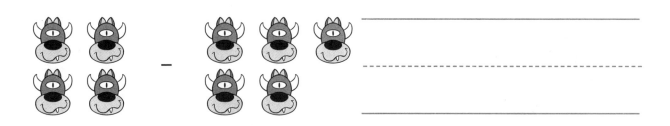

3.

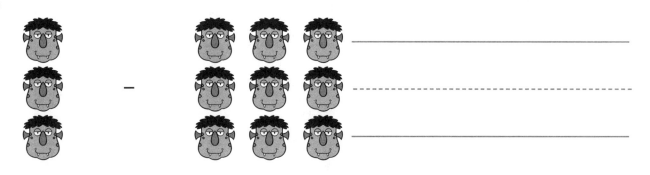

4.

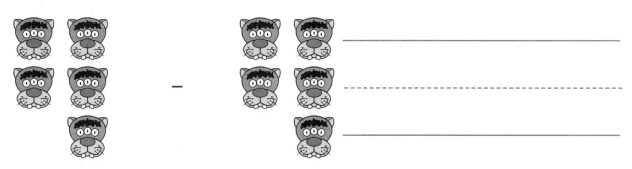

Do More: Read each subtraction sentence aloud.

SOMETHING'S DIFFERENT

Name: _____

Directions: Look at the two pictures below. Can you find all the changes? Circle the things that have changed.

Monster Math Grade 1

94

Name: _____

Directions: Look at the flower at the left. Then, look at the flower on the right. Tell how each flower has changed.

left	right

1.

_____

- - - - - - - - - - - - - - - - - - - -

_____

2.

_____

- - - - - - - - - - - - - - - - - - - -

_____

3.

_____

- - - - - - - - - - - - - - - - - - - -

_____

4.

_____

- - - - - - - - - - - - - - - - - - - -

_____

Monster Math Grade 1

Name: _____

Directions: Draw the monster. Change three things about the monster in your drawing. You can make it shorter or taller, change its clothes, or change its color. You can think of your own changes, too. Show your monster to a friend. Explain what changes you made to the monster.

Do More: Draw 2 monsters. Change 3 things about the first monster to make the second monster. Ask a friend to find the changes.

Name: _____

Directions: Read each change and color the number that shows how that change happened. Use cubes to help.

1. I used to have 5, but now I have 8. How did it change?

+ 3	+ 2	− 3

2. I used to have 12, but now I have 6. How did it change?

− 7	+ 6	− 6

3. I used to have 4, but now I have 9. How did it change?

+ 5	− 5	+ 3

4. I used to have 2, but now I have 7. How did it change?

− 5	+ 4	+ 5

5. I used to have 10, but now I have 6. How did it change?

+ 4	− 4	+ 3

Do More: Make up your own clues for two changes. Have a friend tell how the numbers changed.

Name: _____

Directions: Listen to each funny story about change. Write an addition or subtraction sentence to solve each problem.

1. The monster princess keeps her 8 rubies in her closet. She found 3 more rubies in her left shoe. How many rubies does she have now?

_____

- -

_____

2. Last year, Oscar Monster won 6 trophies for playing soccer. This year, Oscar won 3 more trophies. How many trophies does he have now?

_____

- -

_____

3. Pealer the Monster used to have 12 spots, but his mother scrubbed him too hard in the bath and washed off 5 spots. How many spots does he have now?

_____

- -

_____

4. Bessie the Monster had 7 fancy dresses. The dry cleaners ruined 2 of the dresses. How many dresses does Bessie have now?

_____

- -

_____

5. Buster Monster used to run into 3 stop signs on his way to the park. Somebody put up 5 more stop signs. How many stop signs are there now?

_____

- -

_____

6. Pierre Monster used to have 2 copies of his driver's license. He made one more copy to keep in his wallet. How many copies does he have now?

_____

- -

_____

Directions: Answer the questions to review the skills you have learned.

1. Find the pattern. Draw the next three shapes in the pattern.

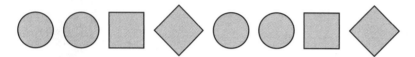

2. Find the pattern. Make the same pattern using colors.

1 1 2 5 1 1 2 5 1 1 2 5

☐ ☐ ☐ ☐ ☐ ☐ ☐ ☐ ☐ ☐ ☐ ☐

3. Write **+** or **−** to make each sentence true.

a. 6 ◯ 2 = 4   d. 10 ◯ 5 = 5

b. 3 ◯ 4 = 7   e. 6 ◯ 3 = 9

c. 9 ◯ 5 = 4   f. 5 ◯ 7 = 12

4. Write **>**, **<**, or **=**.

a. 5 ◯ 9   d. 8 ◯ 7

b. 10 ◯ 10   e. 6 ◯ 3

c. 2 ◯ 8   f. 3 ◯ 3

5. Write an addition or subtraction sentence to solve each problem.

   a. Seven monsters went to a ball. Four of the monsters were wearing sneakers. How many monsters were not wearing sneakers?

    _____

    -

    _____

   b. Eight monsters were playing basketball. Two more monsters came to play. How many monsters were playing basketball altogether?

    _____

    -

    _____

6. Circle the things that have changed.

7. Read the clues and circle the mystery numbers.

   a. I am > 3. I am < 6. What numbers could I be?

    1 2 3 4 5 6 7 8 9 10 11 12 13 14 15

   b. I am > 9. I am < 14. What numbers could I be?

    1 2 3 4 5 6 7 8 9 10 11 12 13 14 15

Name: _____

Directions: Answer the questions.

1. Chito and Miguel Monster went to a pet store. Chito chose 5 fish. Miguel chose 4 fish. How many fish did they buy **all together**?

a. Draw the fish. Count all the fish.

Chito   **Miguel**

_____   _____

- - - - - - - -   - - - - - - - -

b. Write a number sentence. 5 + _____ = _____

2. Angela ate 3 cookies. Cary ate 4 cookies. How many cookies did they eat **all together**?

| 1 | 2 | 3 | 4 | 5 | 6 | 7 | 8 |

a. Start on 3 and **count forward** 4 spaces. You will end _____

- - - - - - - -

at number _____.

_____   _____   _____

- - - - - - -   - - - - - - -   - - - - - - -

b. Write a number sentence. _____ + _____ = _____

HOW MANY ALL TOGETHER?

Name: _____

Directions: Answer the questions.

Materials: counting blocks

1. There are 5 monsters playing soccer. Then, 6 more monsters join them. How many monsters are playing soccer **all together**?

    a. Use counting blocks. Put 5 blocks in front of you. These are the first monsters. Choose 6 more blocks and add them to your pile. These are the other monsters. Count all the blocks.

      _____

      - - - - - - - - - - - - - - -

      There will be _____ monsters all together.

      _____   _____   _____

      - - - - - - - - - -   - - - - - - - - - -   - - - - - - - - - -

    b. Write a number sentence. _____ + _____ = _____

2. Cho Monster eats 2 apples every day for lunch. In one school week, how many apples will she eat **all together**?

    Monday   Tuesday   Wednesday   Thursday   Friday

    Draw 2 apples for each day of the week. Count the apples.

      _____

      - - - - - - - - - - - - - - -

    Cho Monster ate _____ apples all together.

Monster Math Grade 1

Name: _____

Directions: Answer the questions.

1. Kessie's rabbit had 6 babies. She finds homes for 3 of the babies. How many baby rabbits are **left**?

a. Cross out the 3 rabbits that have homes. Count the rabbits that are left.

_____

- - - - - - - - - - - - - - -

There are _____ rabbits left.

_____

- - - - - - - - - - - - - - -

b. Write a number sentence. 6 – 3 = _____

2. Dave has 8 trucks. He gives three old trucks to his little brother. How many trucks does he have **left**?

1	2	3	4	5	6	7	8

Start at 8 on the number line. **Count back** 3 spaces.

_____

- - - - - - - - - - - - - - -

Dave has _____ trucks left.

Directions: Answer the questions.

Materials: counting blocks

1. Al has 19 marbles. He sold 14 to his friend. How many marbles does Al have **left**?

    a. Use counting blocks. Count out 19 blocks. Add 14 blocks or take away 14 blocks? Count the blocks now.

        _____

        Al has _____ marbles left.

        _____   _____   _____

    b. Write a number sentence. _____ − _____ = _____

2. Theo has a box of 14 chocolates. Christa eats 5 chocolates. How many chocolates does Theo have **left**?

    a. Use counting blocks. Count out 14 blocks. Add 5 blocks or take away 5 blocks? Count the blocks now.

        _____

        Theo has _____ chocolates left.

        _____   _____   _____

    b. Write a number sentence. _____ − _____ = _____

Name: _____

Directions: Answer the questions.

Materials: 100 chart

1. I am 1 more than 19. What am I? _____

2. I am 10 more than 10. What am I? _____

3. I am 2 tens and 0 ones. What am I? _____

4. I am 1 less than 100. What am I? _____

5. I am 9 more than 90. What am I? _____

6. I am 9 tens and 9 ones. What am I? _____

Name: _____

Directions: Answer the questions.

Materials: crayons

Group objects in pairs.
Odd numbers will have 1 object left over.
Even numbers will have 0 objects left over.

_____

- - - - - - - - - - - - - - - - -

1. How many monsters all together? _____

2. Match the monsters. Make pairs of monsters the same color.

_____

- - - - - - - - - - - - - - - - -

3. How many pairs did you make? _____

_____

- - - - - - - - - - - - - - - - -

4. Is there a leftover monster? _____

_____

- - - - - - - - - - - - - - - - -

5. Is there an **even** or an **odd** number of monsters? _____

Monster Math Grade 1

Directions: Answer the questions.

Half means make into 2 equal groups.

1. Ann's mother had 6 pencils. She gave **half** the pencils to Ann and **half** the pencils to his brother Gan.

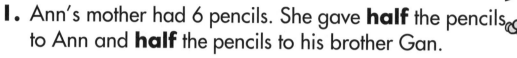

   a. Color Ann's pencils red. Color Gan's pencils green.

   _____   _____

   ---------------   ---------------

   b. How many pencils does An have? _____ Gan? _____

   _____

   ----

   c. What number is **half** of 6? _____

2. Bruce and Lisa's grandmother gave them 8 quarters. She told them to divide the quarters in half.

   a. Circle Bruce's quarters. Put a box around Lisa's quarters.

   _____   _____

   ---------------   ---------------

   b. How many quarters does Bruce have? _____ Lisa? _____

Directions: Answer the questions.

Double means add the same amount again.

1. There are 5 triangles. How many triangles will there be if the amount is doubled?

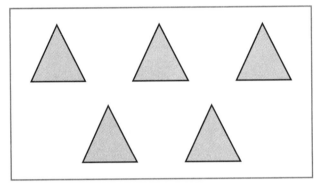

Draw 5 more triangles in the empty box. Count all the triangles.

_____

- - - - - - - - - - -

Finish the number sentence. 5 + 5 = _____

2. What number is 4 doubled?

_____

- - - - - - - - - -

a. Use the number line. Start on 4. Count ahead _____ spaces.

_____ _____ _____

- - - - - -   - - - - - -   - - - - - -

b. Write a number sentence. _____ + _____ = _____

Monster Math Grade 1

Name: _____

The number cruncher uses rules to change numbers. Put a number **IN** and a different number comes **OUT**.

Directions: Use the rule. Fill in the chart. Look for a pattern.

1.

Rule: + 2

Number IN	1	2	3	4	5
Number OUT	3	4			

2.

Rule: + 2

Number IN	2	4	6	8	10
Number OUT	5	7			

NUMBER SHRINKER

Name: _____

The number shrinker uses rules to change numbers. Put a number **IN** and a different number comes **OUT**.

Directions: Use the rule. Fill in the chart. Look for a pattern.

1.

Rule: – 1					
Number **IN**	10	8	6	4	2
Number **OUT**	9	7			

2.

Rule: – 2					
Number **IN**	10	8	6	4	2
Number **OUT**	8	6			

Monster Math Grade 1

Directions: Answer the questions.

These shapes are **squares**.

I. How many sides does
a square have?

_____

- - - - - - - - - - - - - - - - - -

_____

2. How many corners does
a square have?

_____

- - - - - - - - - - - - - - - - - -

_____

- -

3. Which has more sides, a triangle or a square? _____

These shapes are **rectangles**.

4. How many sides does
a rectangle have?

_____

- - - - - - - - - - - - - - - -

_____

5. How many corners does
a rectangle have?

_____

- - - - - - - - - - - - - - - -

_____

ALL ABOUT CUBES

Name: _____

Directions: Answer the questions.

These solid shapes are **cubes**.

A solid shape has **faces** instead of sides. Hold a cube.

_____

- -

1. How many faces does a cube have? _____

_____

- -

2. What shape are the faces? _____

_____

- -

3. How many corners does a cube have? _____

_____

- -

4. How is a cube different from a square? _____

_____

- -

_____

Monster Math Grade 1

Name: _____

Directions: Answer the questions.

These solid shapes are **spheres**.

1. Hold a sphere. Tell what a sphere looks like.

_____

- -

_____

_____

- -

2. How are circles and spheres similar? _____

- -

_____

_____

- -

3. How are circles and spheres different? _____

_____

- -

_____

Name: _____

Directions: Answer the questions.

1. Jenny Monster's birthday party started at 1:00.

  a. Show this time on the clock.

  b. The party ended at 4:00. Show the time on the clock.

  c. How many hours did the party last?

    _____

    - - - - - - - - - - - - - - - - -

    _____

Start Time

End Time

2. Eric Monster's soccer game starts at 10:00.

  a. Show the time on the clock.

  b. After the game, Eric watched his brother's game. He left at 1:00. Show the time.

  c. How many hours was Eric at the soccer field?

    _____

    - - - - - - - - - - - - - - - - -

    _____

Start Time

End Time

Do More: How did you find the number of hours?

Monster Math Grade 1

Name: _____

Directions: Answer the questions.

1. The monster parade started at 9:00 A.M.

   a. Show this time on the clock.

   b. It lasted 2 hours. Show the time the parade ended.

   c. How did you solve this problem?

   _____

   -

   _____

Start Time

End Time

2. Misha Monster went to the park to play. She played for 3 hours with her friends. It was 4:00 when she went home.

   a. Show this time on the clock.

   b. What time did Misha Monster get to the park?

   _____

   - - - - - - - - - - - - - - -

   _____

   c. How did you solve the problem?

   _____

   -

   _____

End Time

Name: _____

Directions: Answer the questions.

Materials: paper clips, centimeter ruler

1. Minnie Monster is running a race. Use small paper clips to measure how far she runs.

   How many paper clips long is the trail?

   _____

   - - - - - - - - - - - - - - - -

   _____

2. Measure the trail using centimeters.

   How many centimeters long is the trail?

   _____

   - - - - - - - - - - - - - - - -

   _____

3. Which way of measuring was easier? Tell why.

   _____

   -

   _____

   _____

   -

   _____

HOW MUCH SPACE?

Name: _____

Directions: Answer the questions.

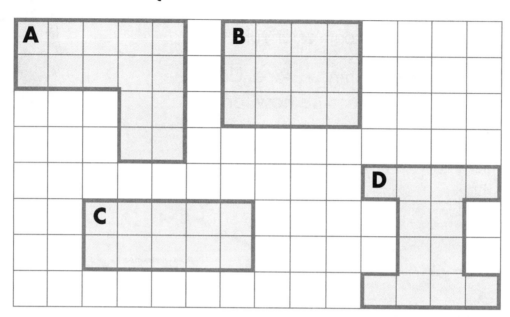

1. Look at the shapes. Estimate.

    a. Which shape has the most space?

    _____

    _____

    b. Which shape has the least space?

    _____

    _____

2. Count the squares in each shape to check your estimates.

_____   _____

-------------------   -------------------

Shape **A**: _____   Shape **B**: _____

_____   _____

-------------------   -------------------

Shape **C**: _____   Shape **D**: _____

Name: _____

Directions: Answer the questions to review the skills you have learned on a separate piece of paper.

1. Robins made nests in Morky Monster's maple tree. Morky climbed the branch of the maple tree. She counted 3 eggs in one nest and 4 eggs in another. How many eggs were there all together?

2. There are an even number of dogs.
There are more than 13 dogs.
There are fewer than 16 dogs.
How many dogs are there?

3. Michael Monster had 12 cookies. His brother ate 7 cookies. How many cookies are left?

4. Double the number of squares. How many squares are there?

5. I have 4 sides. All my sides are equal. What shape am I?

6. I am a solid shape. I have 6 faces and 8 corners. All my faces are equal. What shape am I?

7. The Number Muncher uses rules to change numbers. Look at the rule. Fill in the table.

Rule: + 4

IN:	1	2	3	4	5
OUT:					

Monster Math Grade 1

8. Some monsters were playing on the swings. There were 4 monsters on the jungle gym. There were 9 monsters all together. How many monsters were swinging?

9. Measure the line using paper clips and centimeters.

_____

    a. How many paper clips long is this line?

    b. How many centimeters long is this line?

10. Joel Monster started playing miniature golf at 2:00. He stopped at 5:00. How long did he play?

Start Time   End Time   Time Played:_____

11. Which shape takes up more space? Tell how you know.

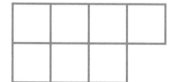 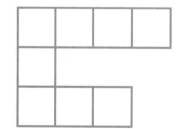

ANSWER KEY

Numbers and Operation

Greater Than, Less Than (1–20) 8
1. >
2. <
3. >
4. <

Greater Than, Less Than (1–20). 9
1. <
2. <
3. >
4. <

One Third 18
1. yes
2. no
3. yes
4. yes
DO MORE: one half

Monster Math Drill 23-24
1. 2, 8, 18, 20
2. 9, 11, 15, 21
3. 18
4. 65
5. 1, 11
6. 9
7. 47
8. Fourteen, pictures will vary.
9. <, >, =
10. Appropriate fraction should be colored in.
11. 16
12. first monster(circled), second monster (box around), third monster (triangle around), fourth monster (crossed out)
13. 4
14. 2

Geometry

Looking for Squares 25
2 squares are colored red.

Looking for Triangles 26
3 triangles are colored blue.

Looking for Rectangles 27
3 rectangles are colored green.

Looking for Circles 28
2 circles are colored orange.

Shapes and Words 30

Siding with a Shape 31
1. 4
2. 3
3. 4
4. 0
5. no
6. 5 inches each

Solid Figures 32
1. cylinder
2. cone
3. rectangular prism
4. cube
5. sphere
6. cylinder

X Marks the Figure 33
X on 2 rectangular prisms, 2 cones, 2 cubes, 1 sphere, and 1 cylinder

ANSWER KEY

Monster Town 34
1. right
2. right
3. left
4. left

Monster Fruit 35
1. left
2. right
3. right
4. right

Above and Below 36
1. 29
2. 43
3. 4
4. 52
5. 39 or 15
6. 13 or 40

Flips 37
1. horizontal flip   2. vertical flip
3. no flip   4. vertical flip

Slides 38

DO MORE: ✖

Turns 39
1. clockwise
2. counterclockwise
3. counterclockwise
4. counterclockwise
5. clockwise

Moving Letters 40

Object Match 41

DO MORE: Drawings will vary.

Name Solid Figures 42
1. cone
2. rectangular prism
3. sphere
4. cylinder
5. cylinder
6. cube

ANSWER KEY

Monster Drill 43–44
1. Student should draw a line.
2. circle
3. 3-dimensional figure
4. fish
5. Student should draw a circle under the rectangle.
6. square
7. flip
8. rectangle

Measurement

Longer and Shorter . . . . .page 45
1. S, L
2. L, S
3. L, S
4. S, L

Merry Monster's Pencil Collection . . . 46
1. Predictions will vary, but proof should include explanation of lining up an actual pencil with the pictures to find that A is the correct answer.
2. Order: E, C, D, B, A
3. Shorter: all

How Much Does It Hold? . . . . . .page 47
1. L, M
2. L, M
3. M, L
4. M, L
5. Answers will vary.

What Is Mass? . . . . page 48
1. 5 wheels
2. shoe
3. pencil
4. book
5. Heavier objects should be on left side.

"Weighting" in Line . . . . .page 49
1. 3, 2, 1 or 3, 1, 2
2. Allow the students to try different methods of comparing the mass of three objects. They may compare two on the balance scale then compare the third object to one of those. Make sure that they recheck their order before recording it. Encourage them to explain the steps of their process in detail.

Counting Units . . . . page 50
1. The pencil is 5 paper clips long.
2. The marbles don't help describe the size of this pencil because they are scattered around.

Units Describe Size . . . . page 51
1. The scissors are 7 blocks long or as long as 7 blocks.
2. The stamps do help because they are lined up.

What Is Area? . . . . .page 52
1. The monster's quilt will have 20 squares. Try to let the students figure out a method they create. If they need help, suggest that they trace the little square on scrap paper and cut out several copies. Or provide 1" cube blocks or connecting cubes or tiles. Make sure they are covering the whole space and not just iterating with a single block.
2. 20

Counting Minutes . . . . page 53
Answers: 1 minute, 5 minutes, 11 minutes, 30 minutes

Monster Measurement . . . . page 54
1. 2
2. 6
3. 5
4. 3

ANSWER KEY

Shape and Area . . . . page 55
1. 12

2-3. Area does not change when the shape is reconfigured. Encourage students to explore this using grid paper and a construction paper shape.

Which Unit? . . . . page 56
1. measuring cup
2. ruler
3. measuring cup
4. balance scale
5. ruler

Measuring in a Jar . . . . page 57
1. yes
2. b
3. yes
4. maybe—hard to tell, rice not level

Students should recognize this as similar to tools used in the kitchen. They should also recognize the need for leveling the top of the material to get an accurate measurement.

Inch by Inch . . . . page 58
1. 5 inches
2. 6 inches

Finding Centimeters . . . . page 59
Students label the things they measure.

Inches and Centimeters . . . . . . page 60
Measurements are approximate.
Stem A: 3 inches/8 cm
Leaf A: 2 inch/5 cm
Stem B: 5 inches/13 cm
Leaf B: 1 inch/3 cm

Days of the Month . . . . page 61
Answers will vary. This activity will help the students recognize that days of the month fall on different days of the week. They won't see many patterns, but they may recognize that if the month begins on a Friday or Saturday, the last day or two will not fit in the calendar grid unless they share a space.

Monster Math Drill . . . . . . .pages 62–63
1. second pencil
2. first foot
3. second monster
4. first glass
5. second marble
6. 3:50
7. eight blocks
9. clock, scale

Data Analysis and Probability
Odd Shape Out 64
1. X is on the fourth circle.
2. X is on the third square.
3. X is on the second triangle.
4. X is on the fourth shape. (5-sides)
DO MORE: Answers will vary.

Doesn't Belong 65
1. Circle the third (legs)
2. Circle the second (spots)
3. Circle the fourth (three eyes)
4. Circle the first (no spots)

Monster Word Sort 66
1. Answers can be any of these words: house, room, work, book, show.
2. house, truck
3. house, cake
4. Answers can be any of these words: cake, work, truck, walk, book.

ANSWER KEY

Data Sets 67
1. 4
2. 3
3. 6
4. 4
5. 4
6. 4

Counting Data 68
Red, 12; Blue, 16; Green, 8; Yellow, 5; Purple, 8

Monster Cookies 69
1. ⅋⅋⅃⅃ ; 5 squares colored
2. ||| ; 3 squares colored
3. |||| ; 4 squares colored
4. ⅋⅋⅃⅃ | ; 6 squares colored
DO MORE: They both show the number in the cookie jar.

Is That a Fact? 70
1. fact
2. opinion
3. opinion
4. opinion
5. fact
DO MORE: Answers will vary.

Monster Facts 71
The signs colored are:
Grapes are a fruit.
Ice is frozen.
Blue is a color.
A fly is a bug.

Apples and Monsters 72–73
DO MORE: 4
1. 2
2. Growly
3. Fuzzy
4. 2
5. Scowly

Monster Pictograph 74–75
DO MORE: Each book stands for 1 book.
1. 8
2. 5
3. 4
4. 5
5. 2
DO MORE: 2

Color Bar Graph 76–77
1. 8
2. 4
3. 9
4. 5
5. blue
DO MORE: 26

The Mode 78
1. 1
2. 4
3. 7
4. 8
5. 14
DO MORE: Answers will vary. Sample answer: 8 is in the list 4 times. 7 is in the list 2 times. 4 is greater than 2.

Middle Number 79
1. 2
2. 6
3. 17
4. 8
5. 112
DO MORE: yes

Is That Possible? 80
1. possible 2. impossible 3. impossible
4. possible 5. impossible
DO MORE: Events will vary.

Monster Math Drill 81–82
1. 4
2. Marlo
3. Sahir and Jimmy
4. 5
5. X is on the small white square.
6. Circle the fish.
7. possible
8. certain

Algebra

The Key to a Monster's Heart 83
"My heart" is the large heart to the right in the middle of the page.

Again and Again and Again 84
1. triangle
2. square
3. circle
4. star

Pattern Synonyms 85
1. Check students' patterns.
2. Have students explain how the two patterns are the same.

Make It Equal 86
Groupings may vary.

More Than One Answer 87
1. Accept any number 1–6.
2. Accept any number 6 or greater.
3. Accept any number 1–8.
4. Accept any number 9 or greater.

Murray's Monster Mystery. 88
1. 5, 6
2. 9, 10, 11, 12
3. 2, 3, 4, 5
4. 7, 8, 9, 10, 11, 12, 13

Mixed Signals. 89
1. <   2. >   3. >   4. <   5. =   6. <

Signs of the Times. 90
1. +   2. +   3. −   4. −   5. +

Monster Skill Check. 91
1. The right side should show 6 blocks in any arrangement.
2. a. +   b. −   c. −   d. +
3. a. >   b. =   c. <   d. >
4. a. 9, 10, 11, or 12   b. 3, 4, 5, or 6

Something's Different. 94
There are now two birds instead of one. The woman on the bike is no longer pulling a baby. The picnic basket is now a trunk. There are 2 girls and a boy playing with the flying disc instead of two boys and a girl. There are now two fawns instead of one. There are trees missing.

Not Quite the Same 95
1. The flower is bigger.
2. The flower is smaller.
3. The flower is shorter.
4. The flower is taller.

Monster Changes. 96
Check drawings.

Monster Stories 98–99
1. 8 + 3 = 11
2. 6 + 3 = 9
3. 12 − 5 = 7
4. 7 − 2 = 5
5. 3 + 5 = 8
6. 2 + 1 = 3

ANSWER KEY

Monster Math Drill 100–101
1. The next shapes are circle, circle, square.
2. Sample colors: blue, blue, red, green.
3. **a.** − **b.** + **c.** − **d.** − **e.** + **f.** +
4. **a.** < **b.** = **c.** < **d.** > **e.** > **f.** =
5. **a.** $7 - 4 = 3$ **b.** $8 + 2 = 10$ **c.** $2 + 5 = 7$
6. The eyebrows and antennae have changed.
7. **a.** 4 or 5 **b.** 10, 11, 12, or 13

Problem Solving

How Many All Together? 102
1. **a.** check drawings **b.** $5 + 4 = 9$
2. **a.** 7 **b.** $3 + 4 = 7$

How Many All Together? 103
1. **a.** 11 **b.** $5 + 6 = 11$
2. 10

How Many Left? 104
1. **a.** 3 **b.** $6 - 3 = 3$
2. 5

How Many Left? 105
1. take away; 5 **b.** $19 - 14 = 5$
2. **a.** take away; 9 **b.** $14 - 5 = 9$

Guess My Number 106
1. 20
2. 20
3. 20
4. 99
5. 99
6. 99

Odd Monsters 107
1. 7
2. Answers will vary.
3. 3 pairs
4. yes
5. odd

Make It Half 108
1. **a.** 3 pencils should be red. 3 pencils should be green. **b.** 3; 3 **c.** 3
2 **a.** 4 quarters should be circled. 4 quarters should be in a box.
  b. 4; 4

Twice as Nice 109
1. $5 + 5 = 10$
2. **a.** 4 **b.** $4 + 4 = 8$

Number Cruncher 110

Rule: + 2					
Number IN	1	2	3	4	5
Number OUT	3	4	5	6	7

Rule: + 2					
Number IN	2	4	6	8	10
Number OUT	5	7	8	10	12

Number Shrinker 111

Rule: − 1					
Number IN	10	8	6	4	2
Number OUT	9	7	5	3	1

Rule: − 2					
Number IN	10	8	6	4	2
Number OUT	8	6	4	2	0

ANSWER KEY

Slick Squares & Rowdy Rectangles . . 112
1. 4
2. 4
3. square
4. 4
5. 4

All About Cubes 113
1. 6
2. squares
3. 8
4. Squares are flat. Cubes are solid. Cubes are made from 6 squares put together.

Spheres 114
1. Spheres are round, solid objects. They have no faces or corners. They roll. They look like a ball.
2. Circles and spheres are both round.
3. Circles are flat. Spheres are solid. They don't have any sides. They are not flat.

Monsters on Time 115
1. **a.** Clock should show 1:00.
b. Clock should show 4:00.   **c.** 3 hours.
2. **a.** Clock should show 10:00.
b. Clock should show 1:00.   **c.** 3 hours.
DO MORE: Answers will vary.

How Long? 116
1. **a.** Time should show 9:00.
b. Time should show 11:00.
c. Count forward 2 hours.
2. **a.** 4:00.   **b.** 1:00   **c.** Count backward 3 hours.

Minnie Monster's Race 117
1. Answers will vary.
2. 33 centimeters
3. Answers will vary.

How Much Space? 118
1. Answers will vary.
2. **A.** 14 squares   **B.** 12 squares
C. 10 squares   **D.** 12 squares

Monster Math Drill 119–120
1. 7 eggs
2. 14 dogs
3. 5 cookies
4. 6 squares
5. square
6. cube
7.

Rule: + 4					
IN:	1	2	3	4	5
OUT:	5	6	7	8	9

8. 5 monsters swinging
9. Answers will vary.; about 9 centimeters
10. 3 hours
11. the second shape; more squares